LETTER A

A A A A

A A A A

a a a a

a a a a

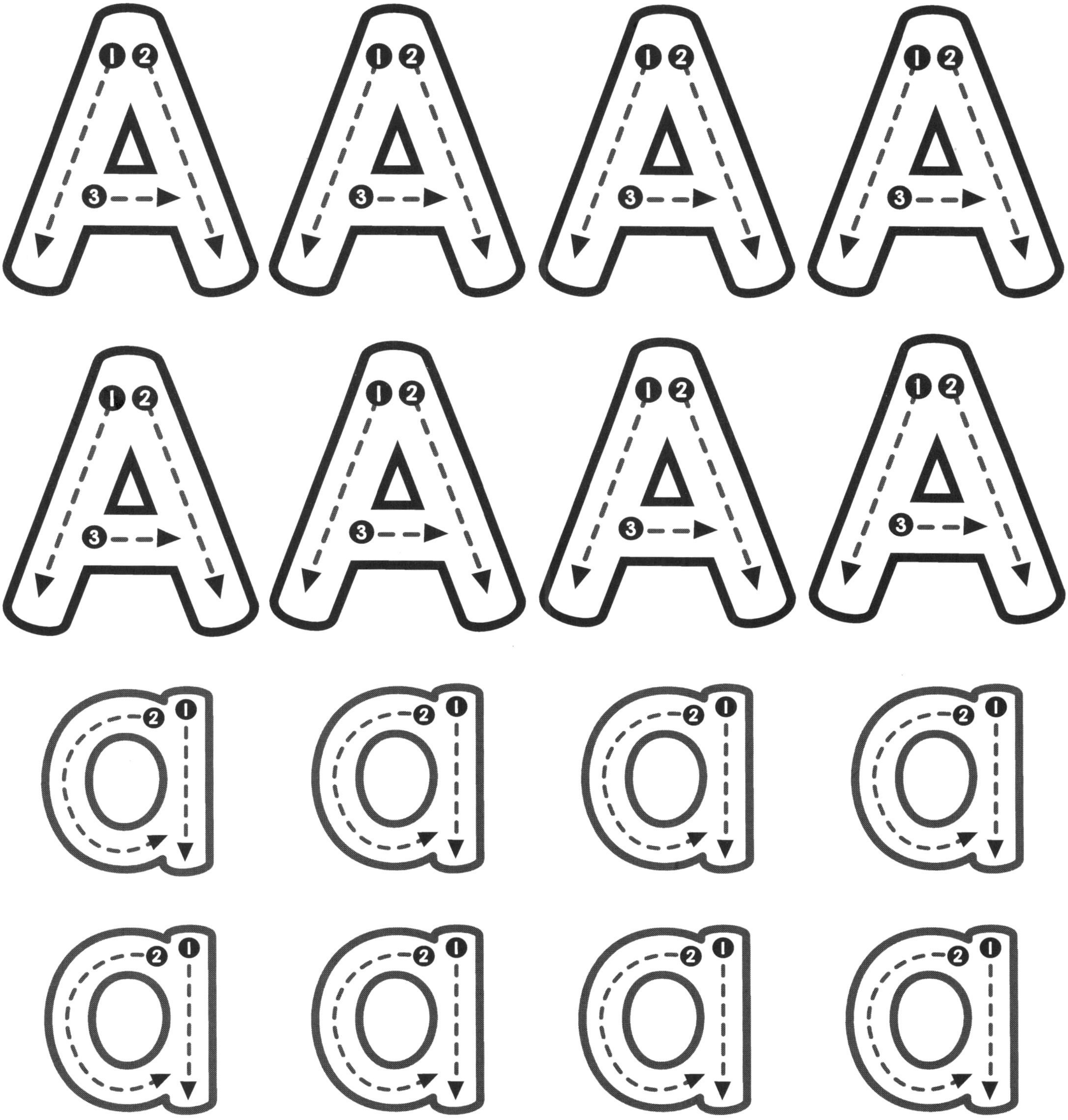

Ant

LETTER B

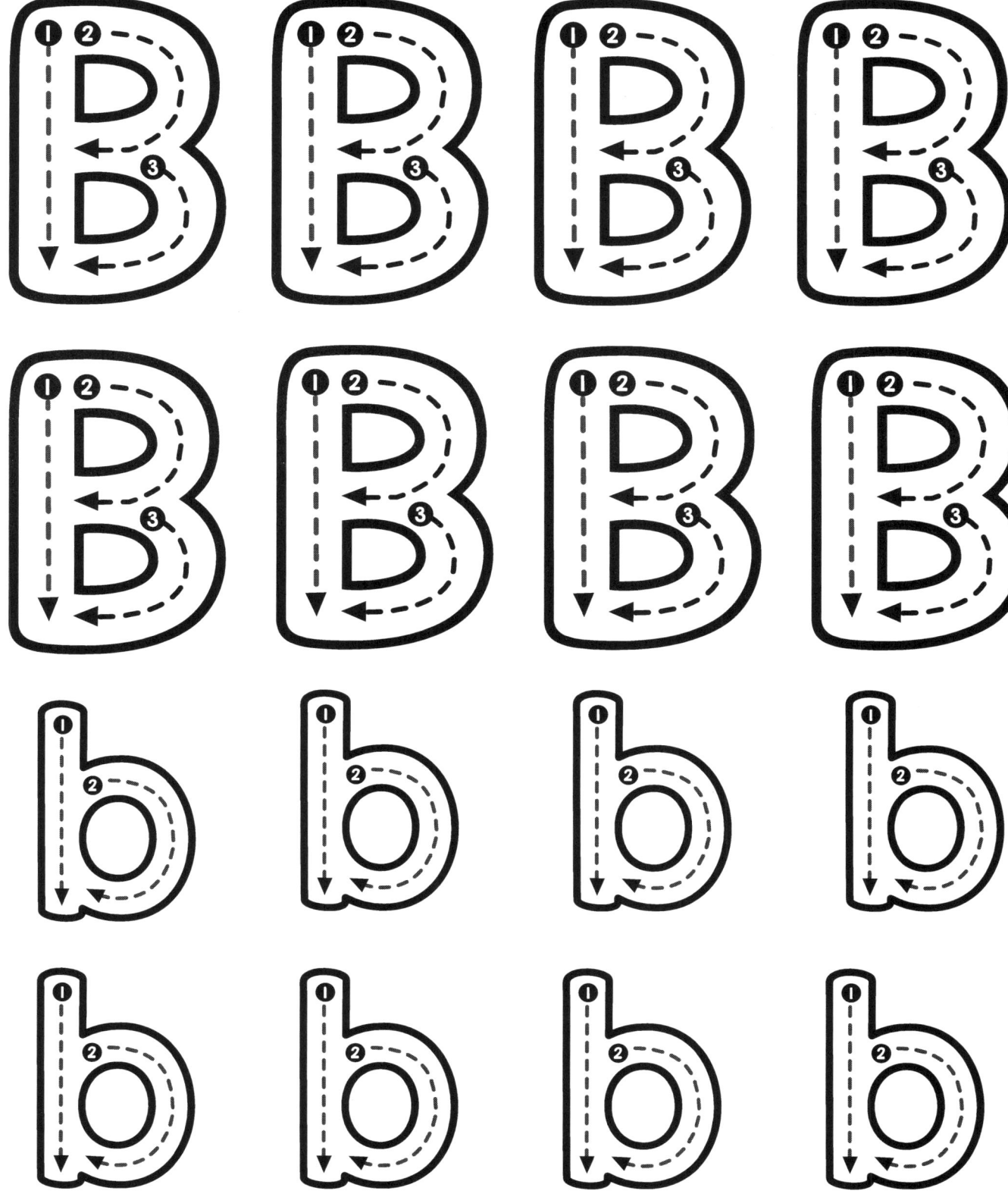

Bird

LETTER C

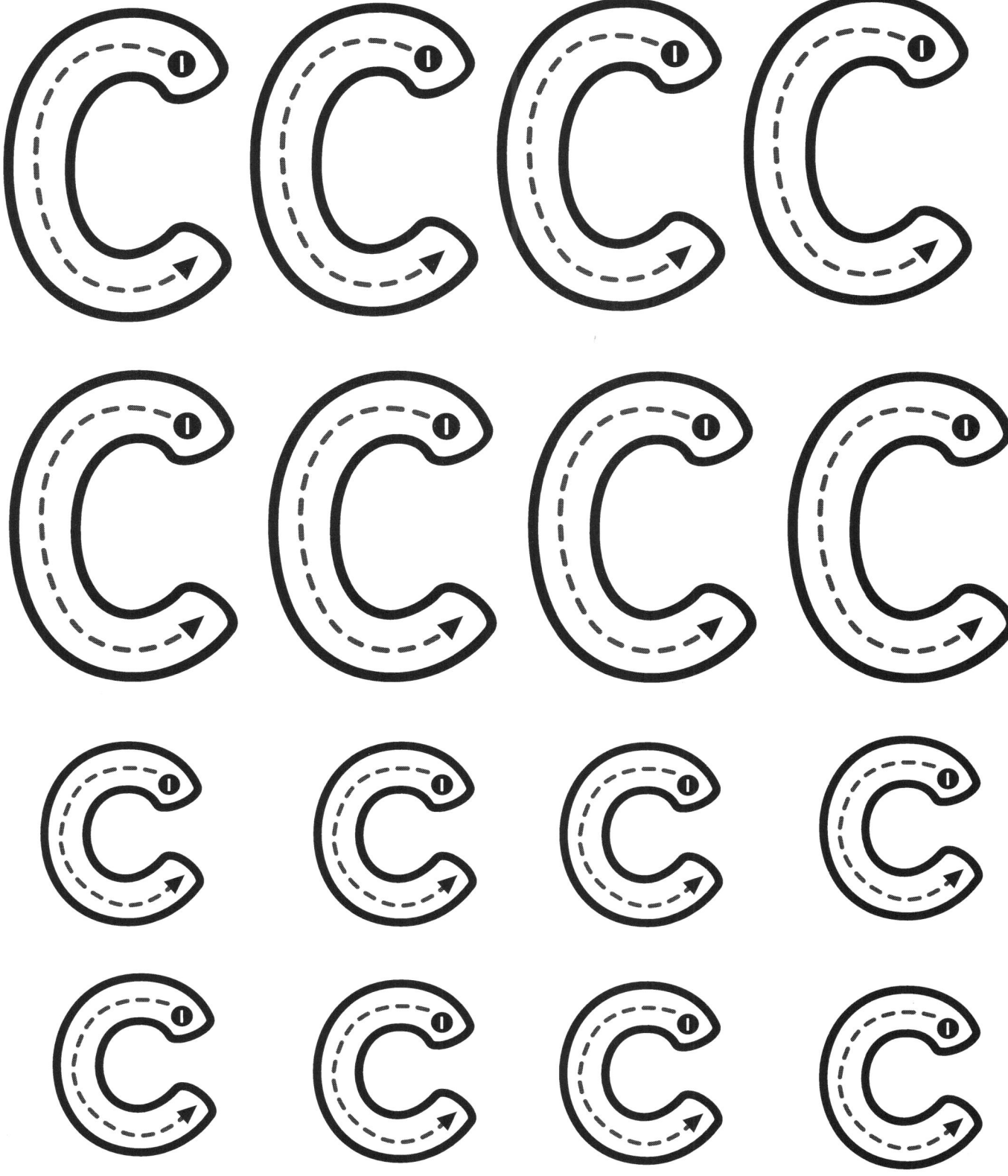

Cow

LETTER D

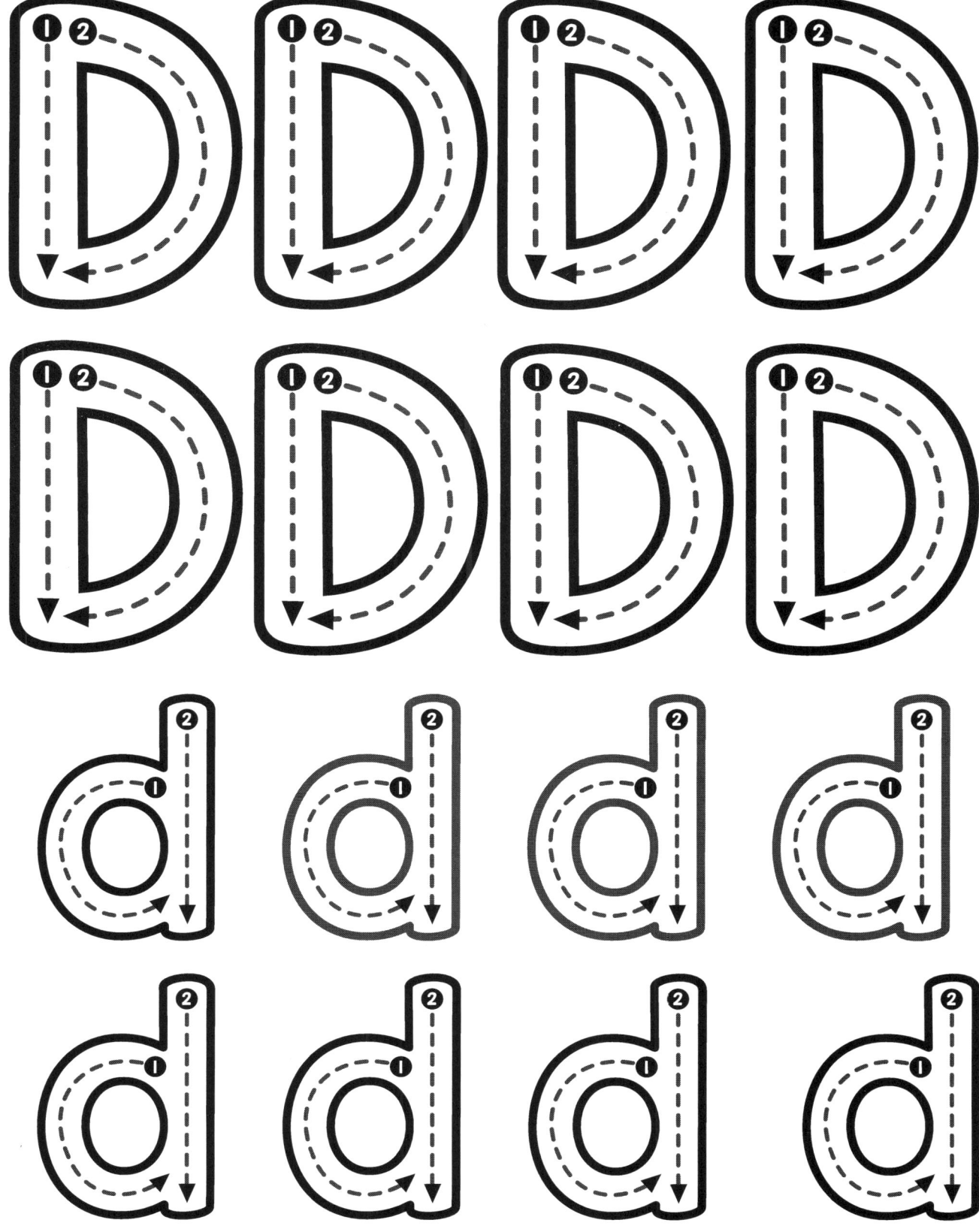

Dog

LETTER E

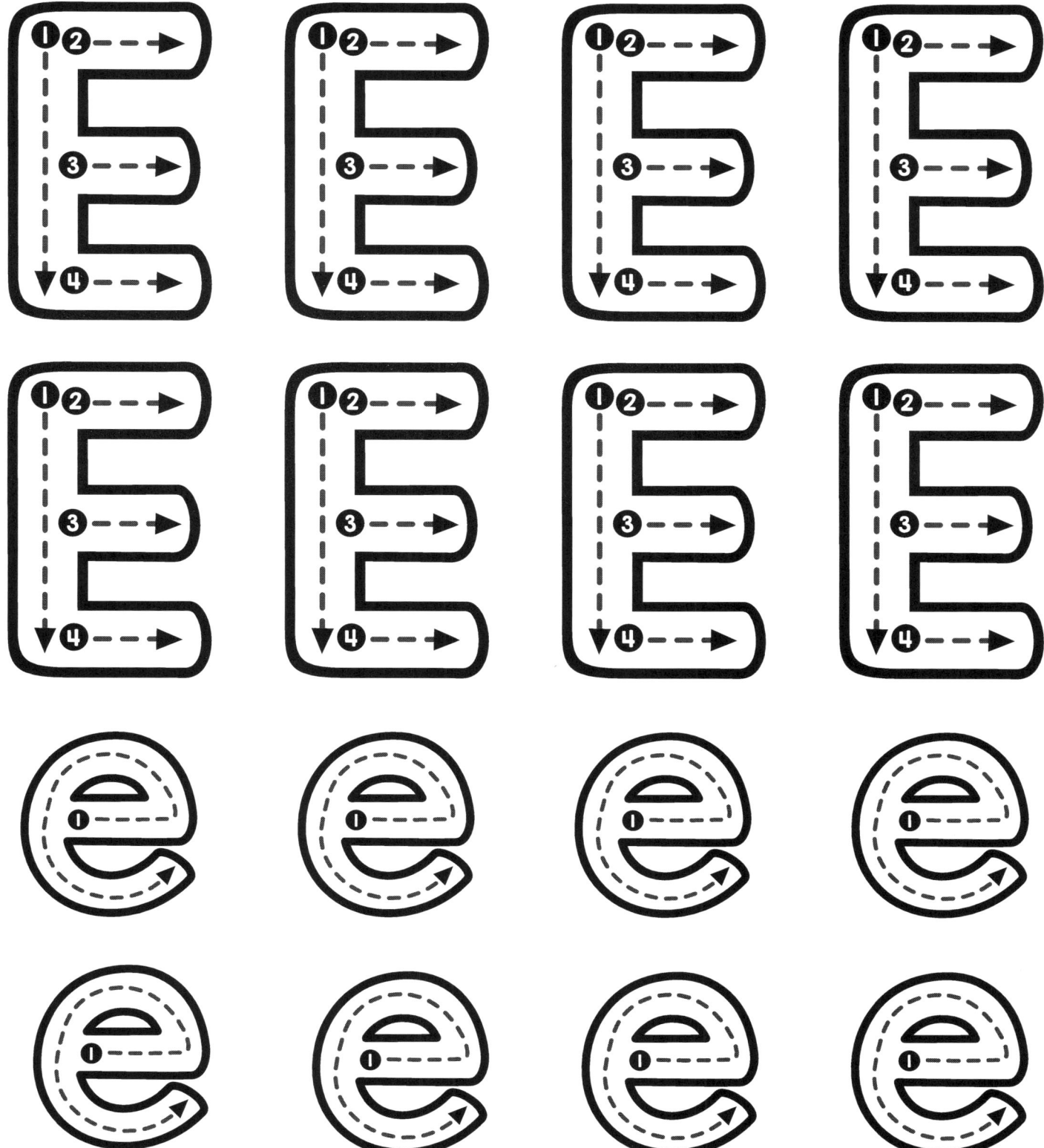

Elephant

LETTER F

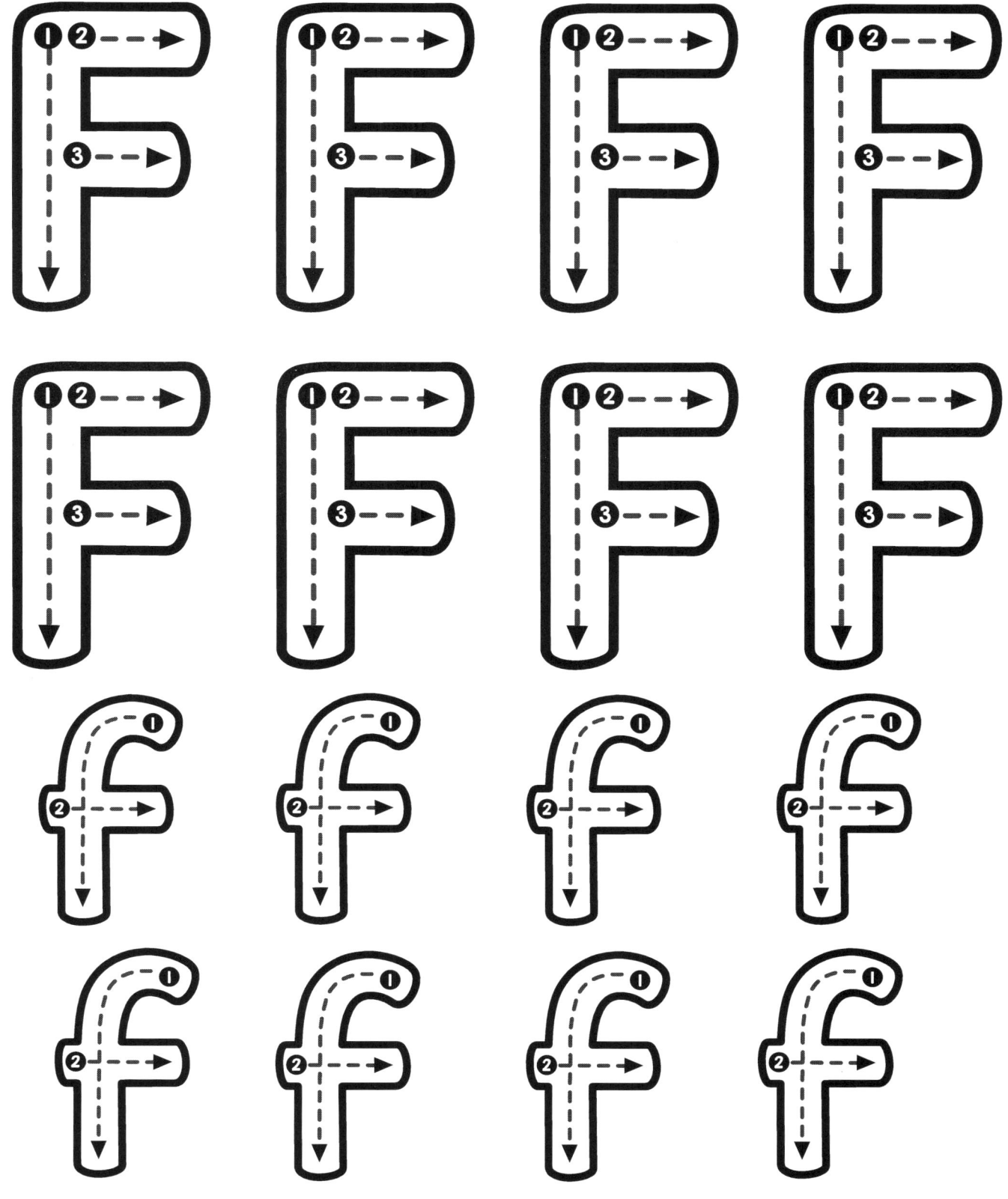

Fox

LETTER G

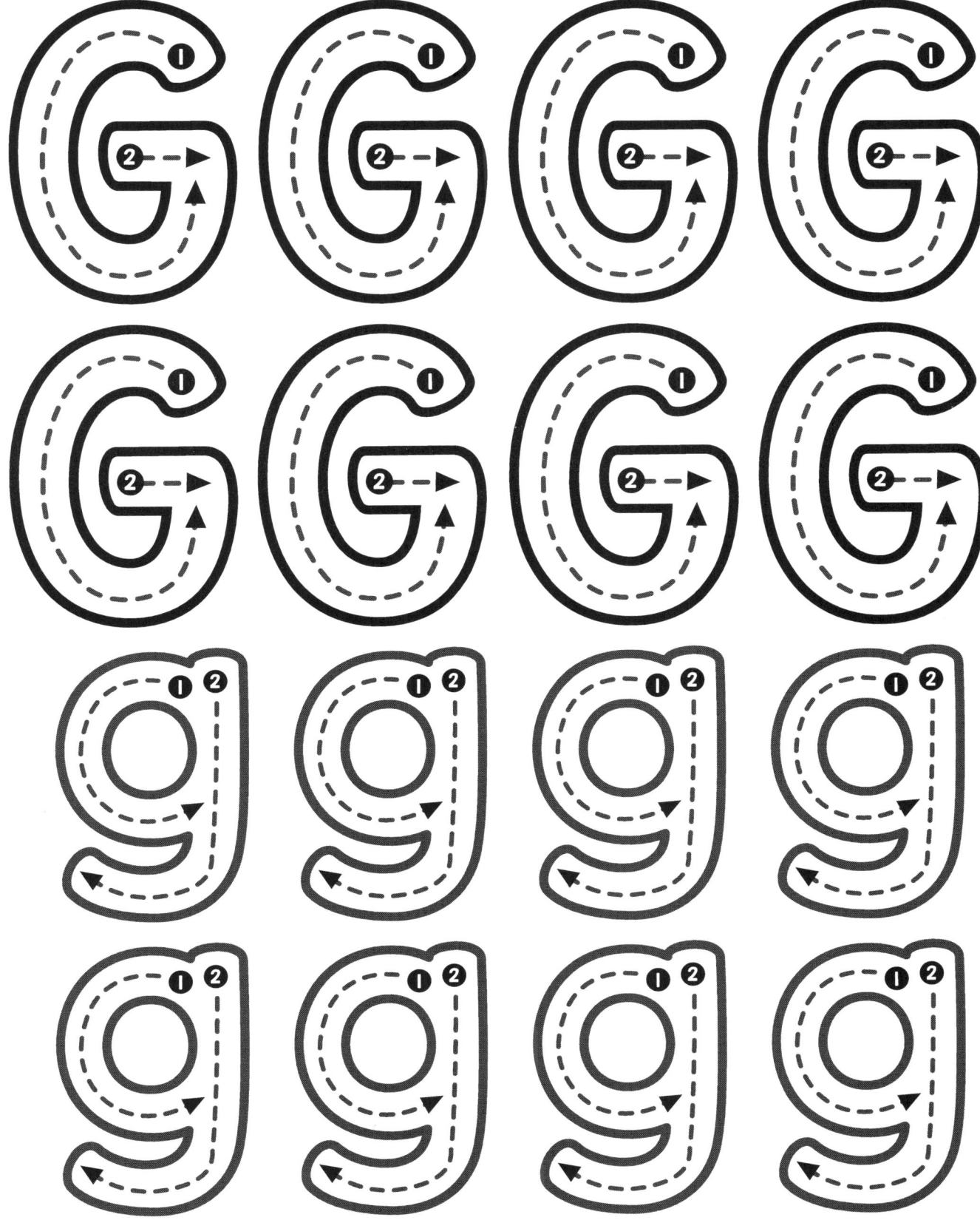

Gorilla

LETTER H

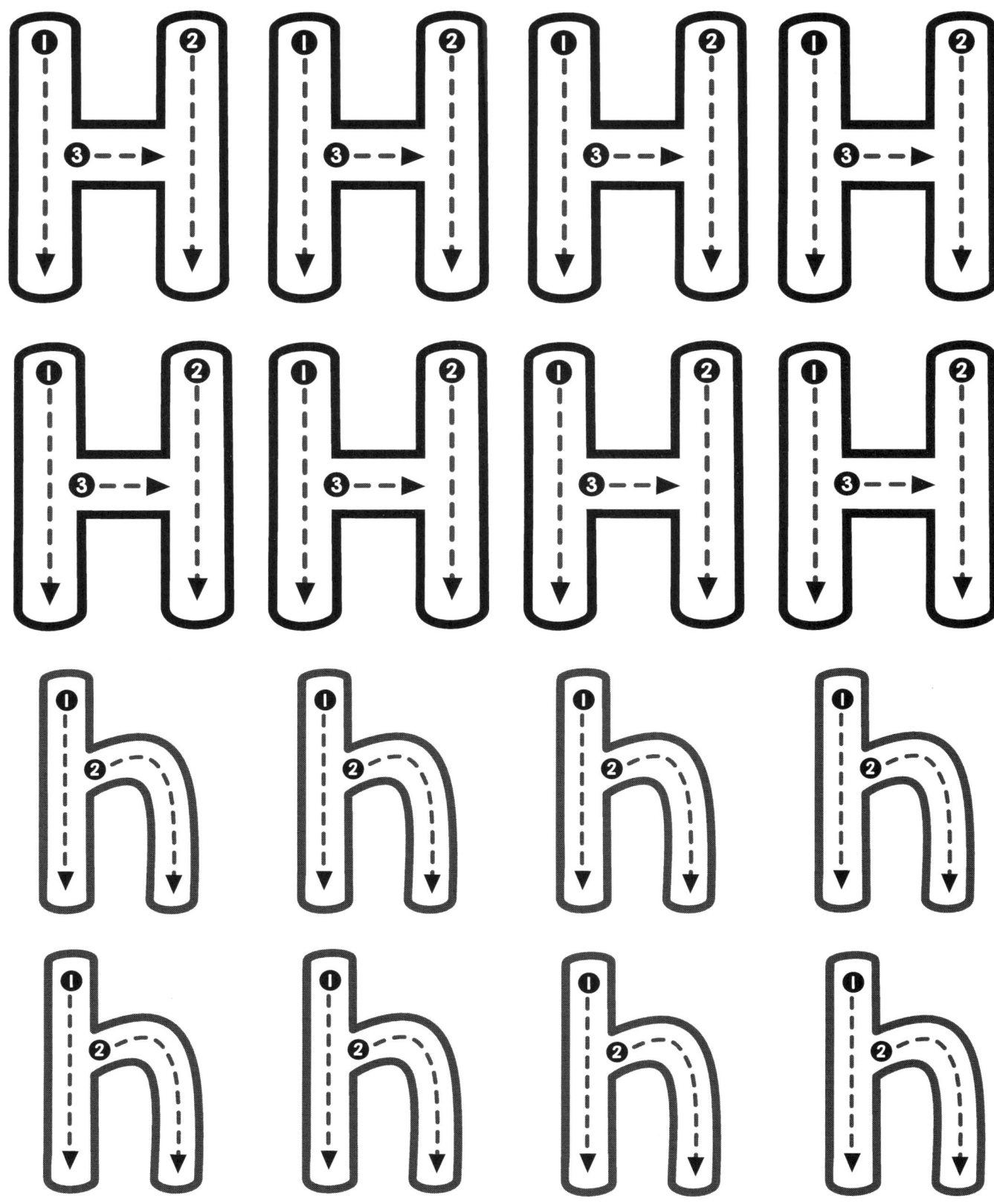

Hippo

LETTER I

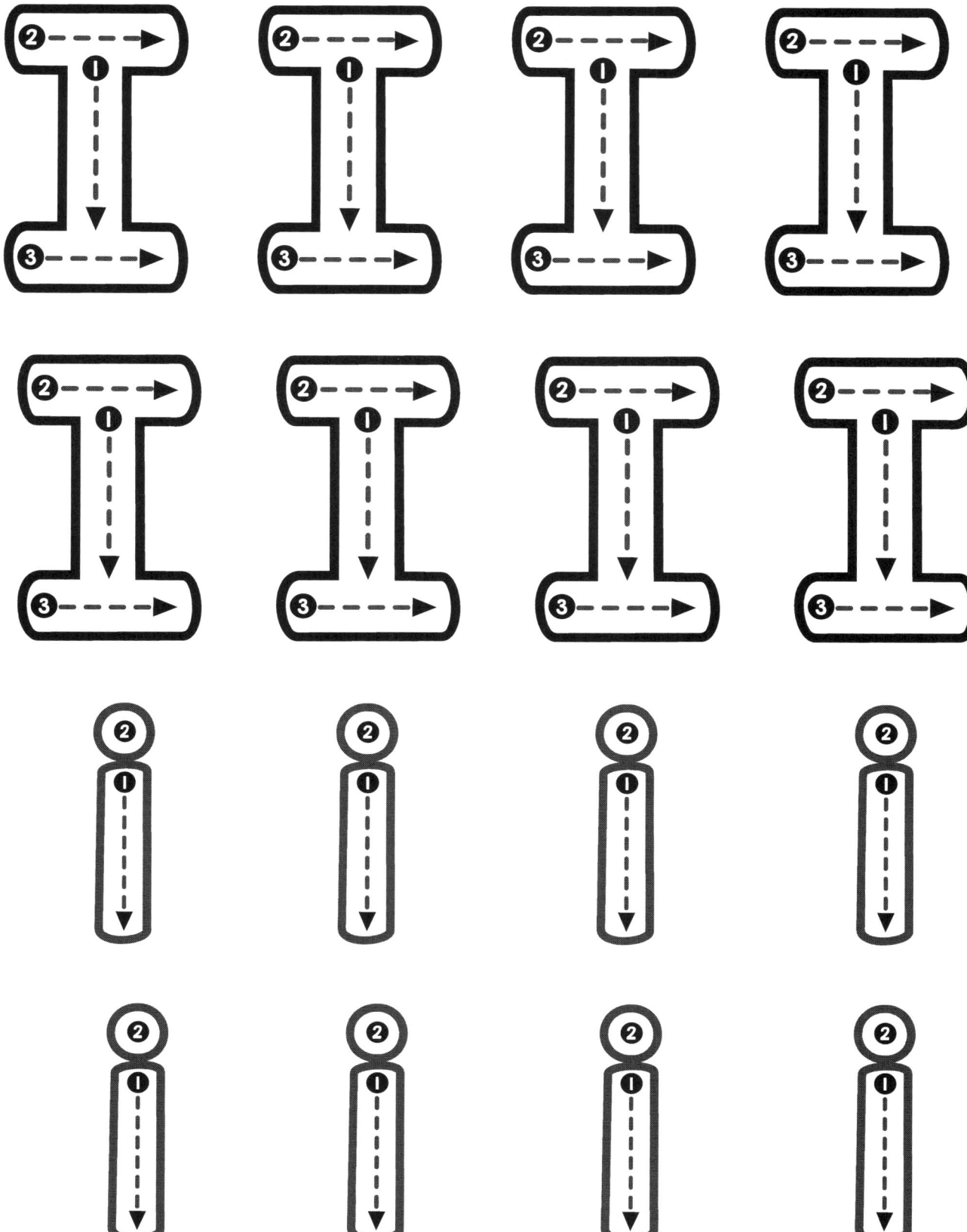

Iguana

LETTER J

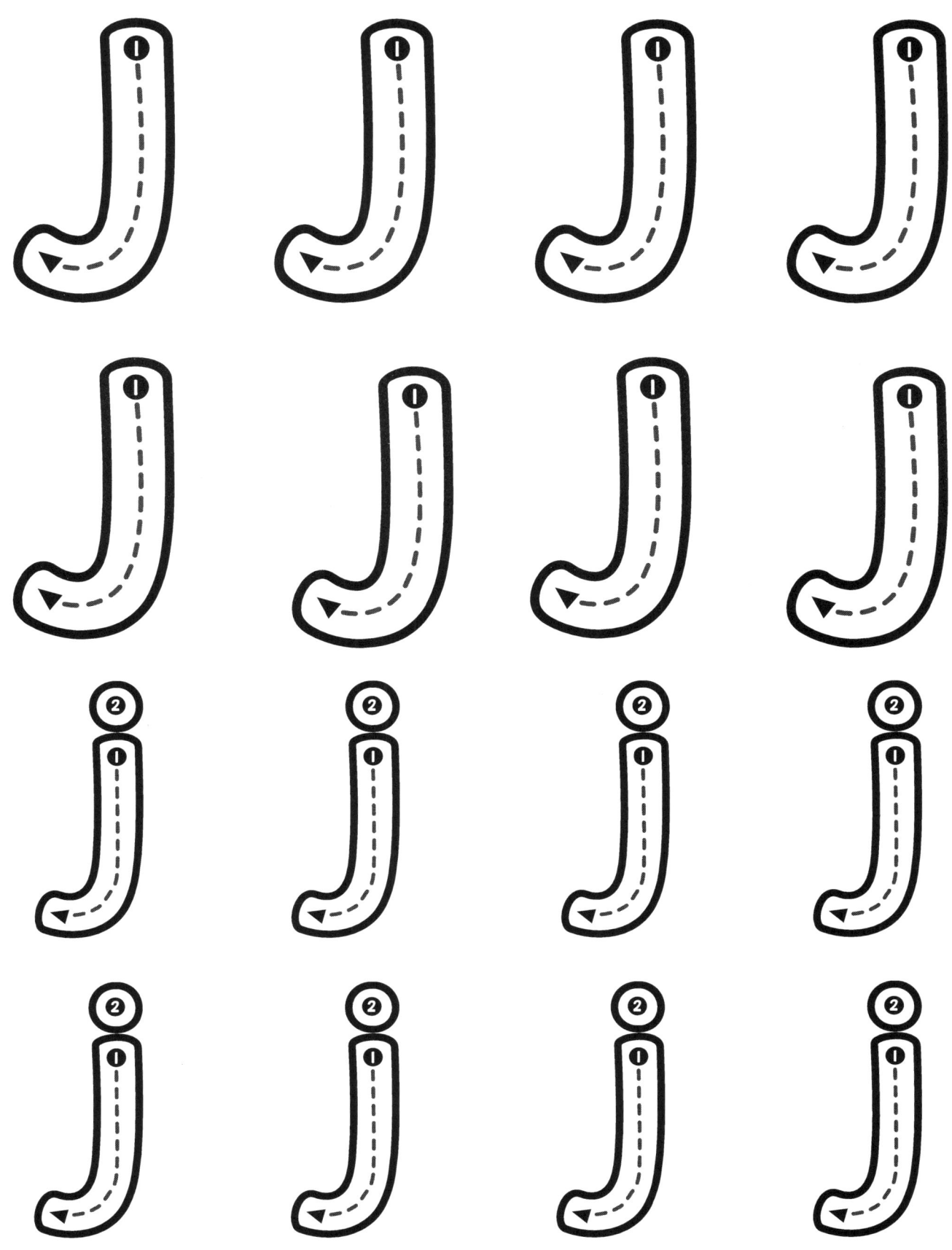

Jellyfish

LETTER K

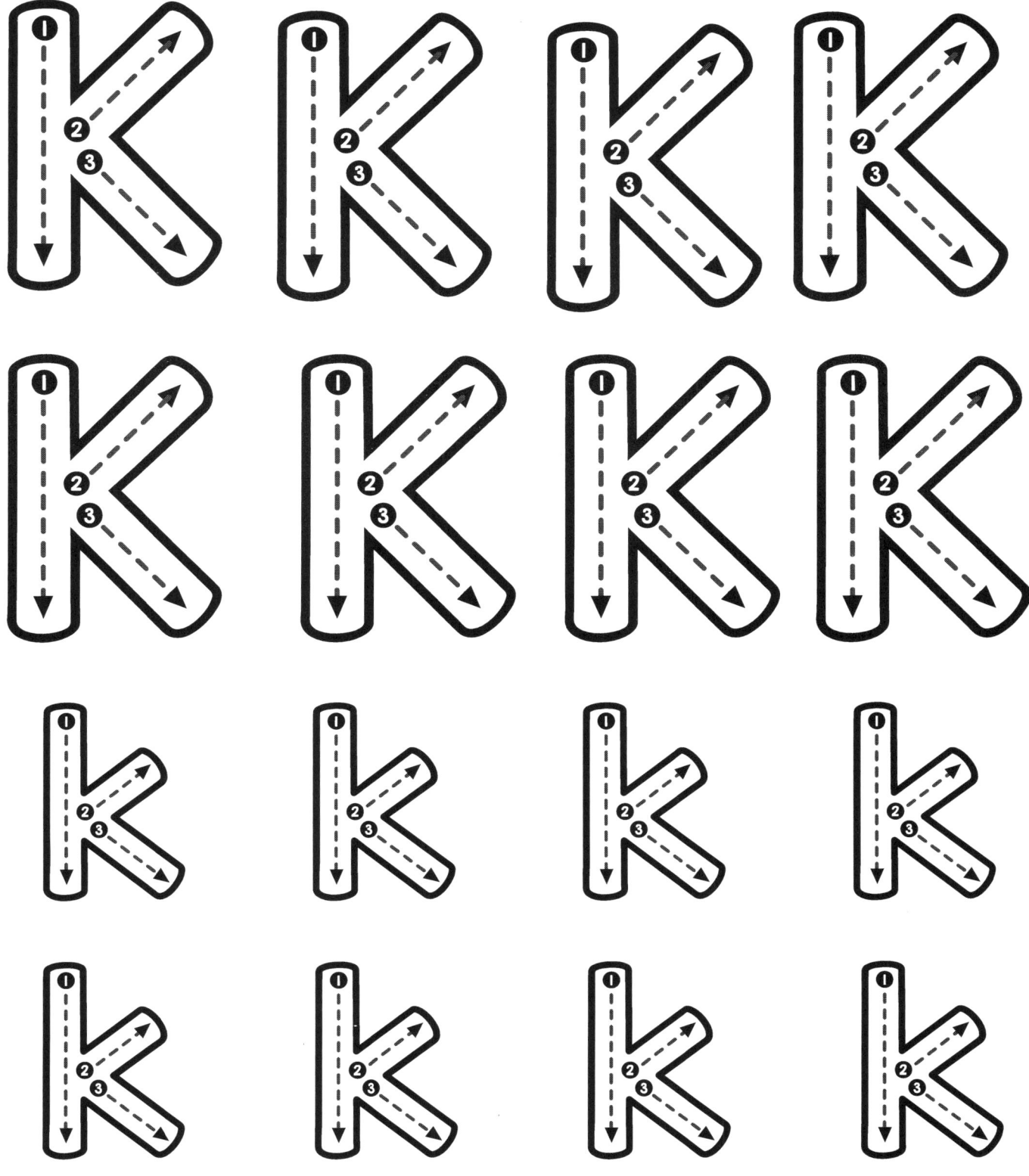

Kangaroo

LETTER L

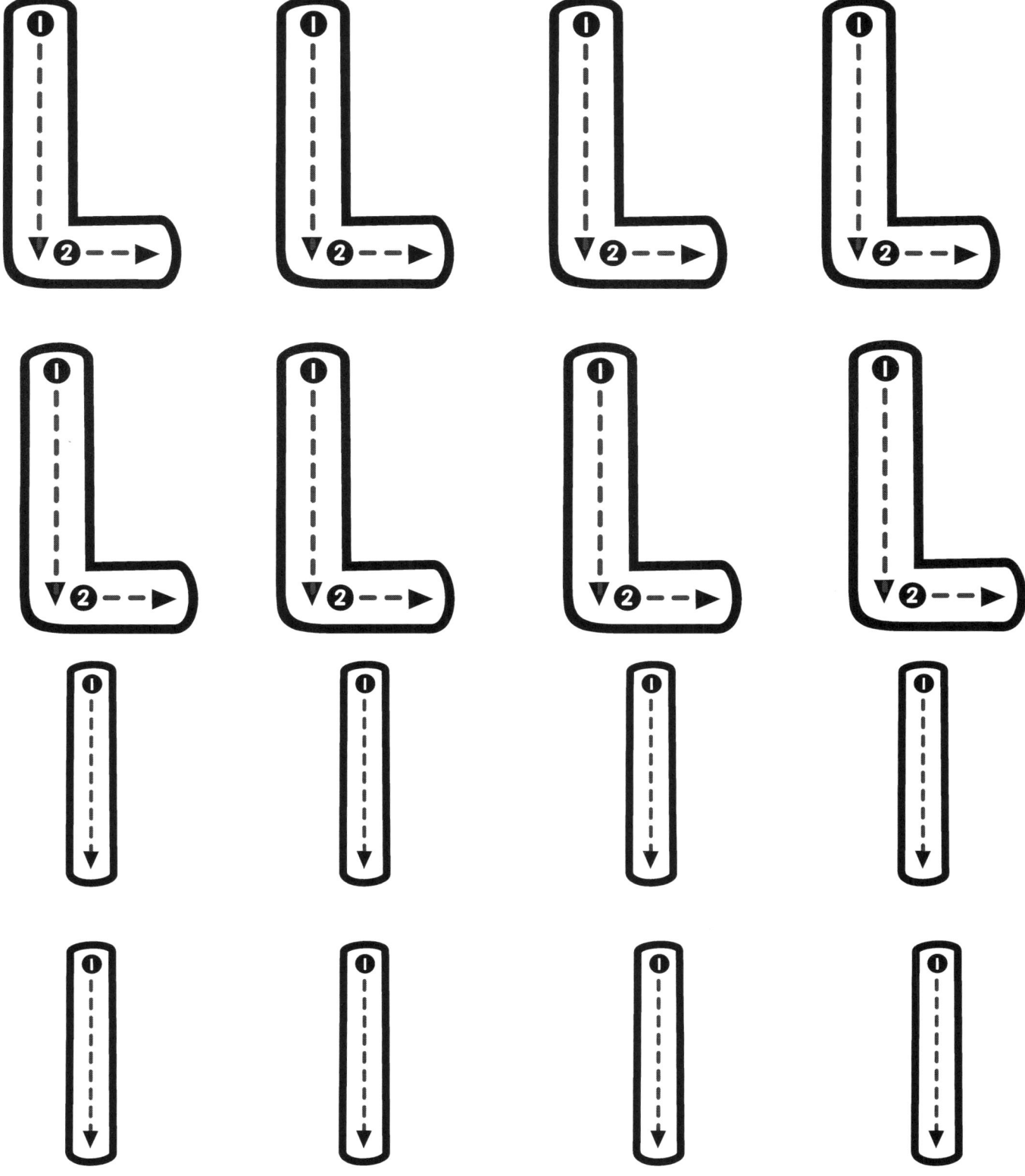

Lion

LETTER M

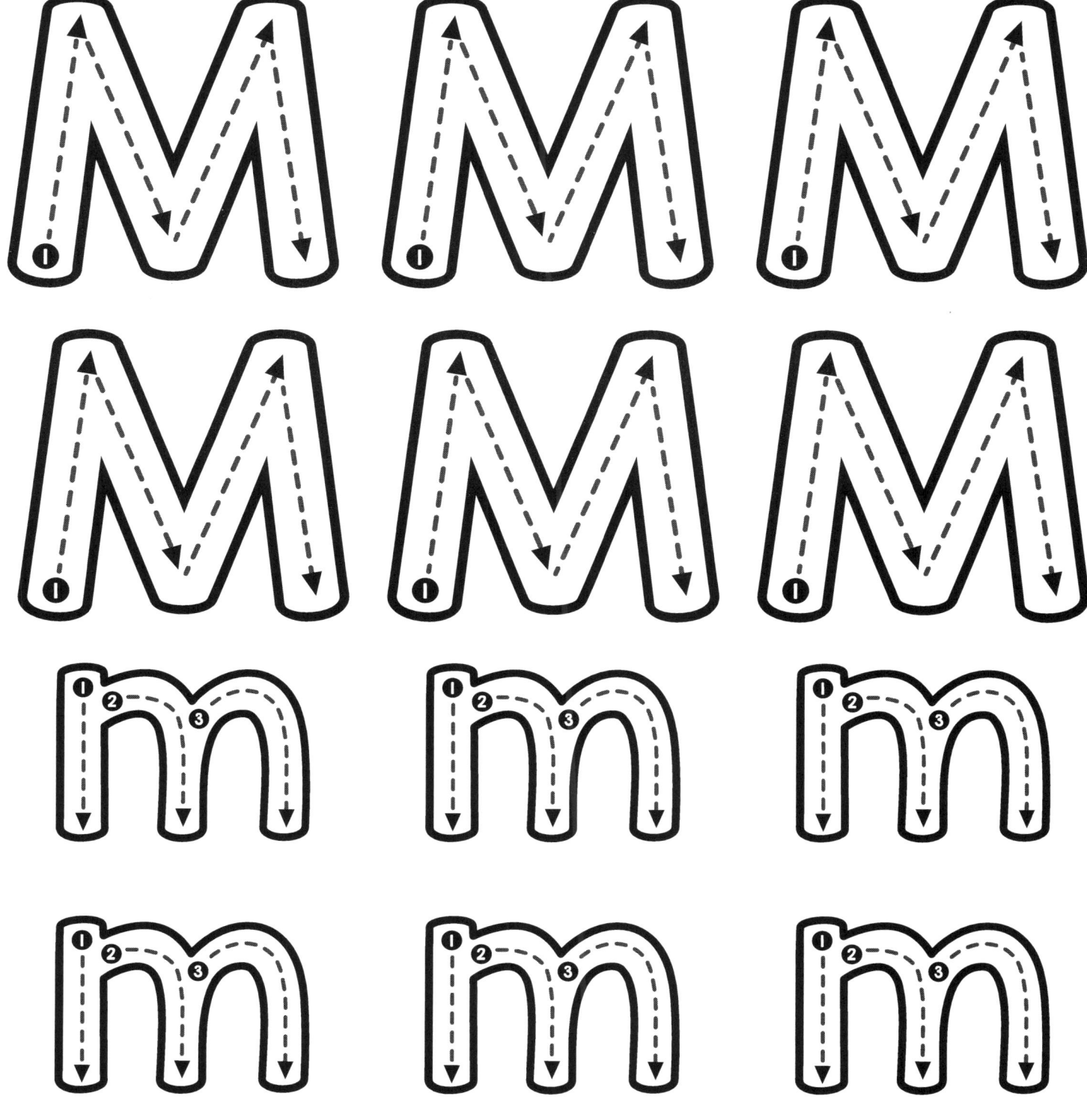

Monkey

LETTER N

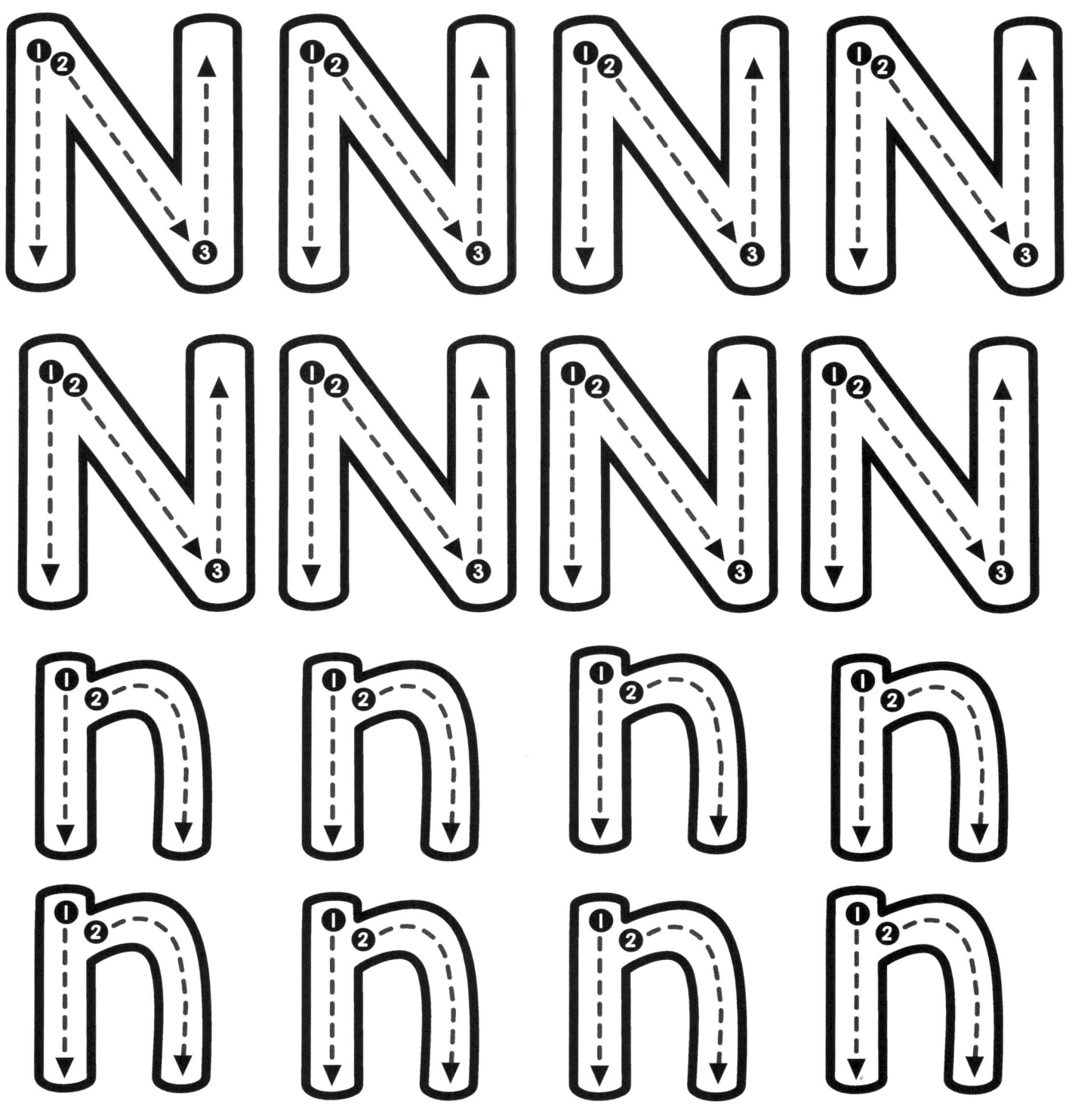

Newt

LETTER O

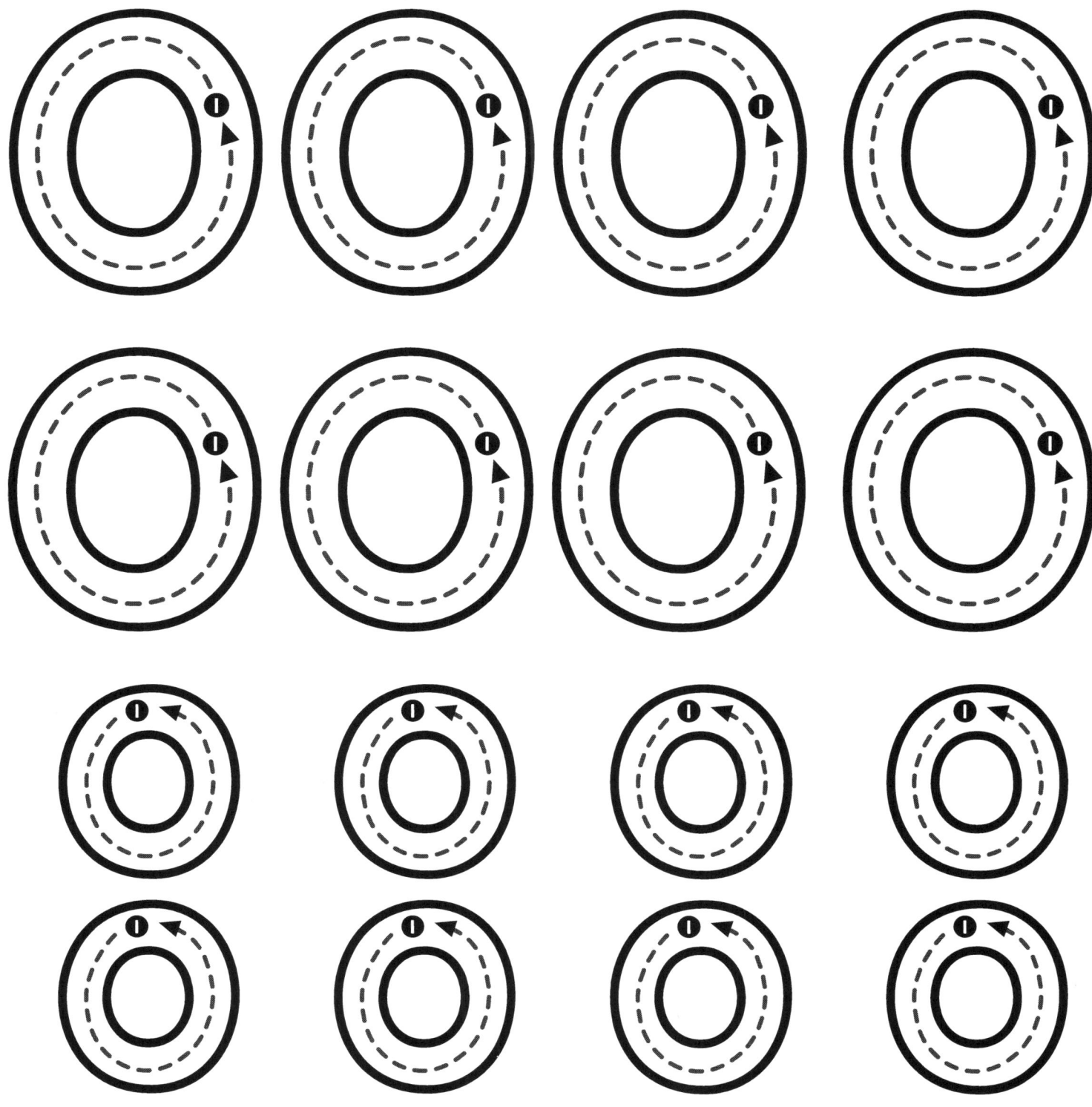

Owl

LETTER P

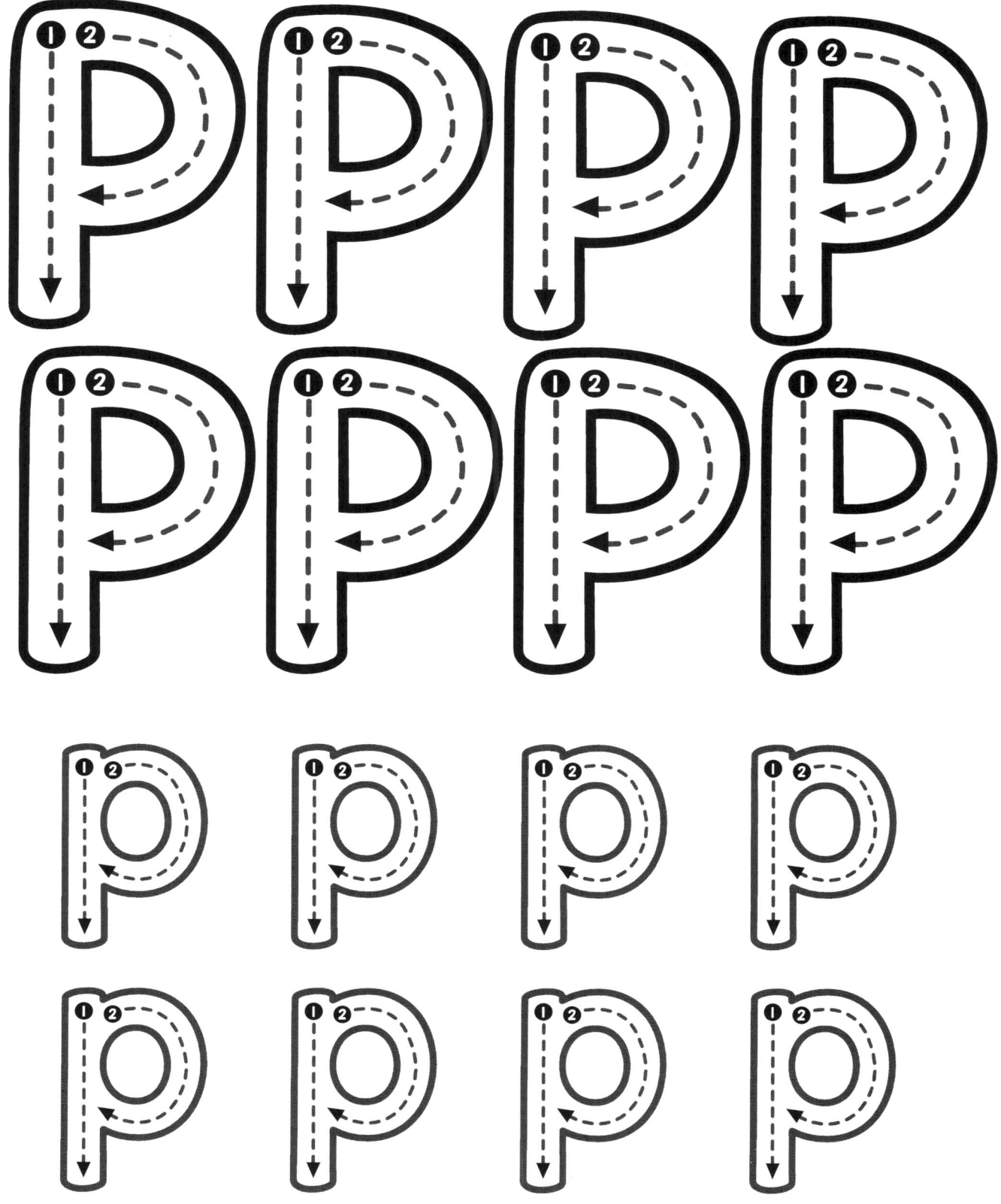

Pig

LETTER Q

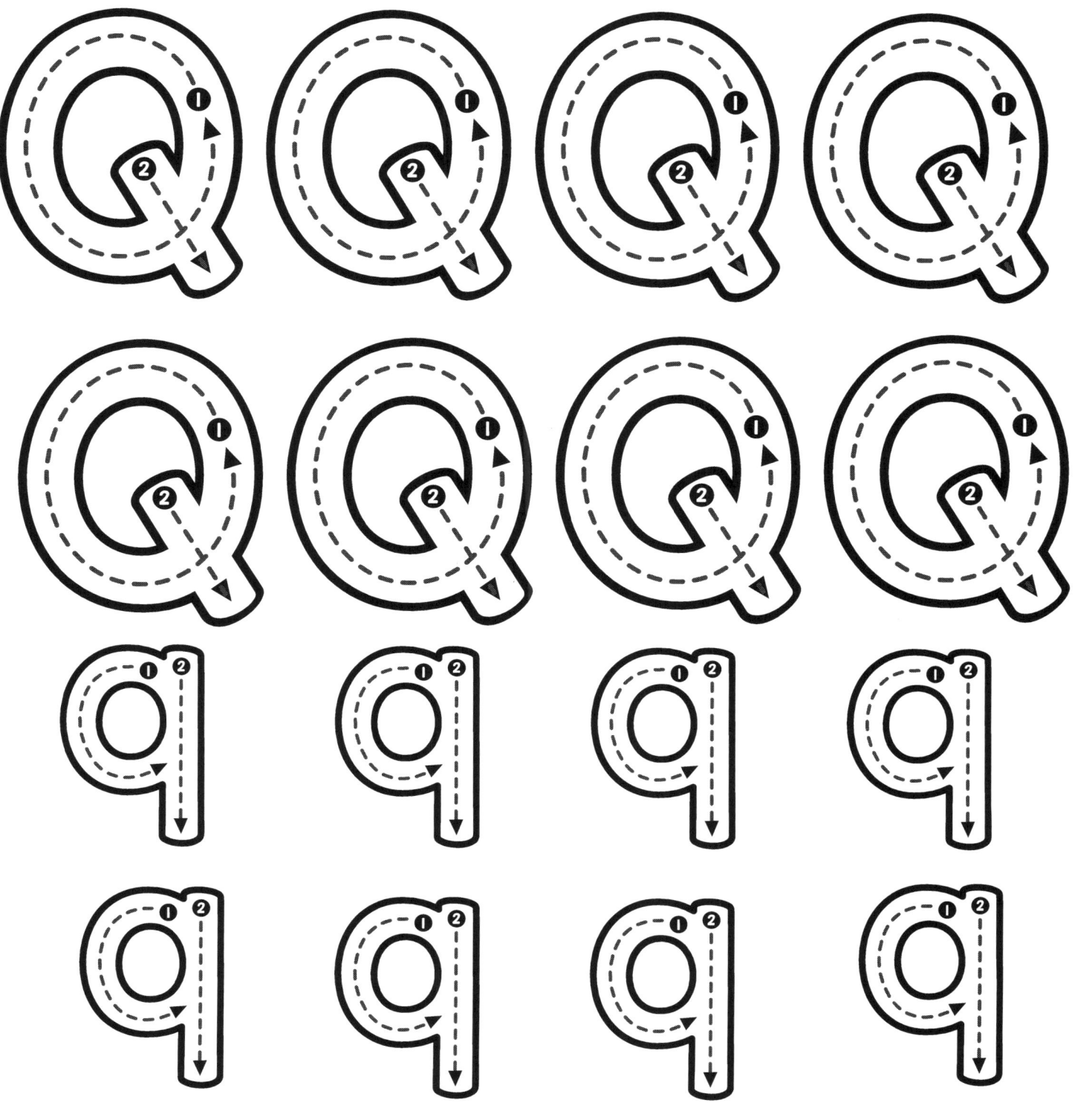

Quail

LETTER R

Rabbit

LETTER S

Snake

LETTER T

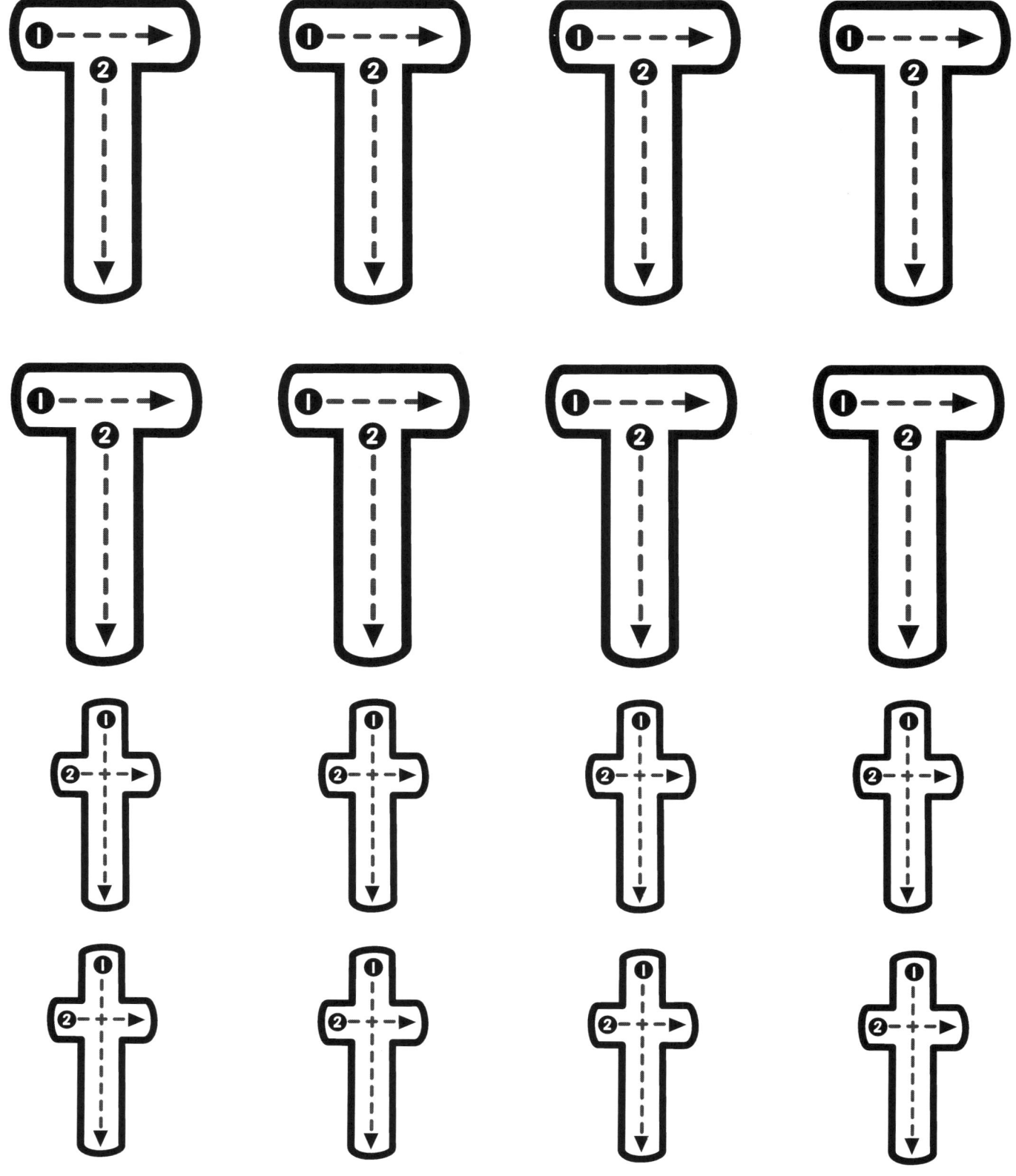

Turtle

LETTER U

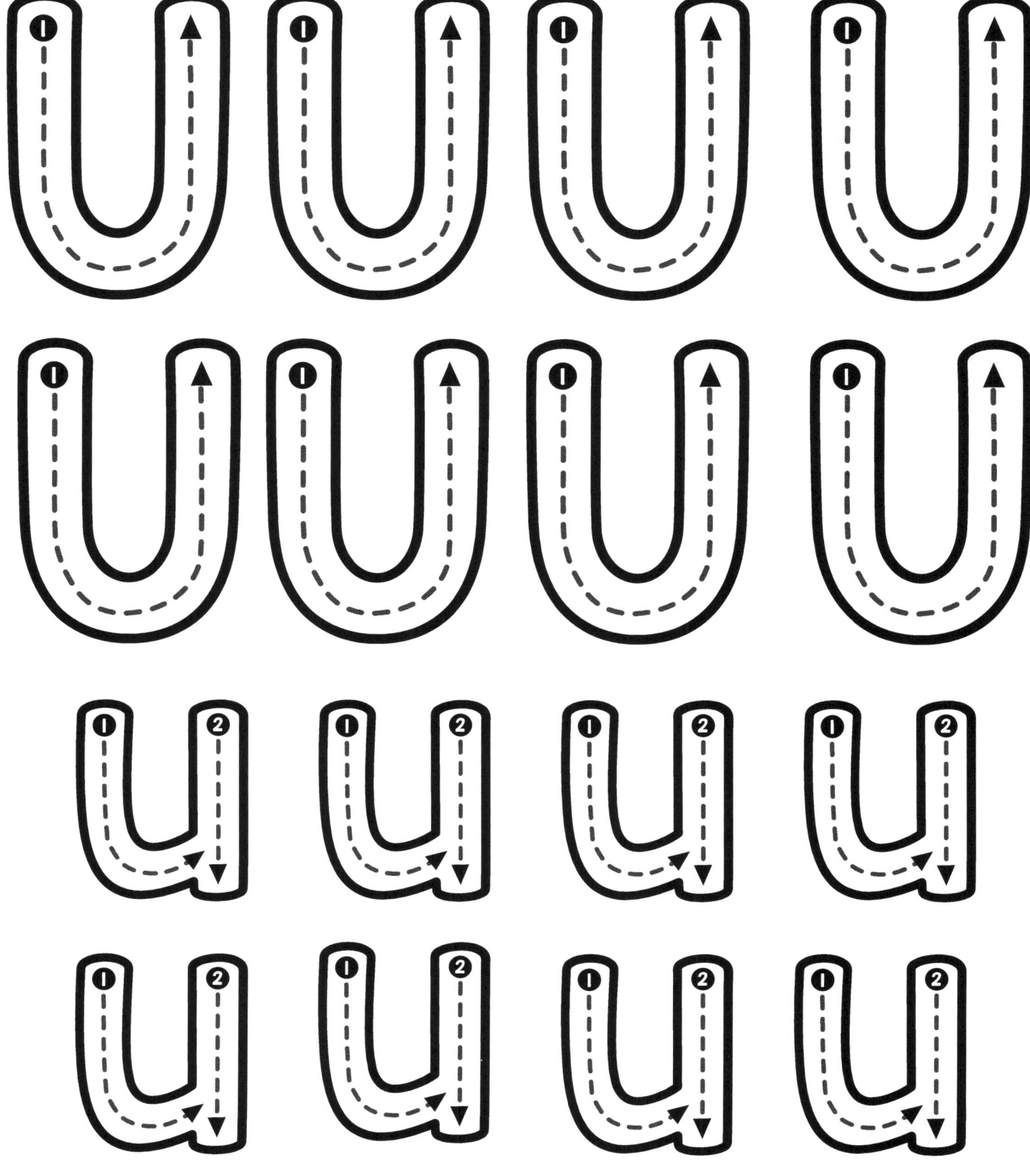

Unicorn

LETTER V

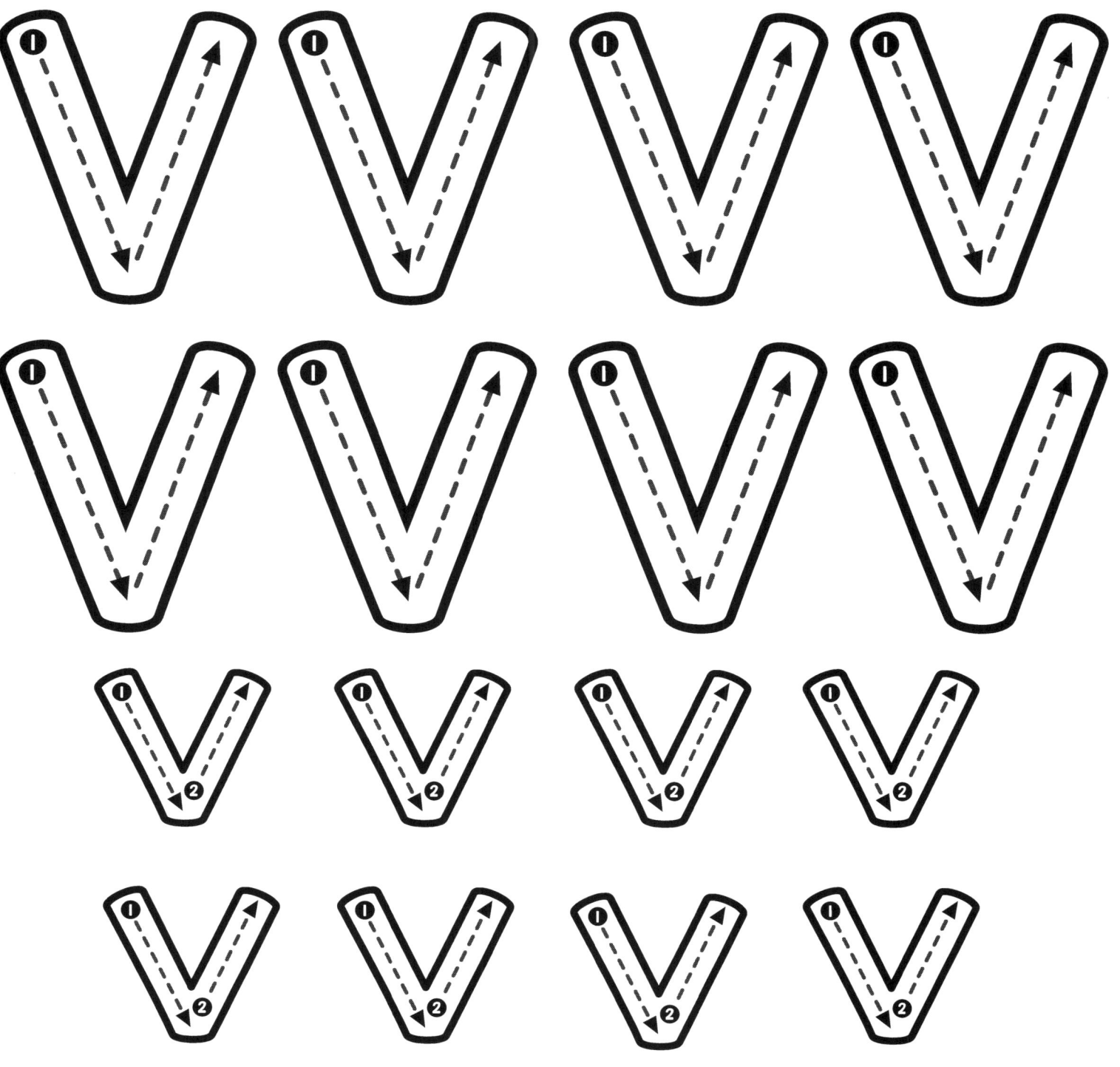

Vulture

LETTER W

Wolf

LETTER X

X-ray

LETTER Y

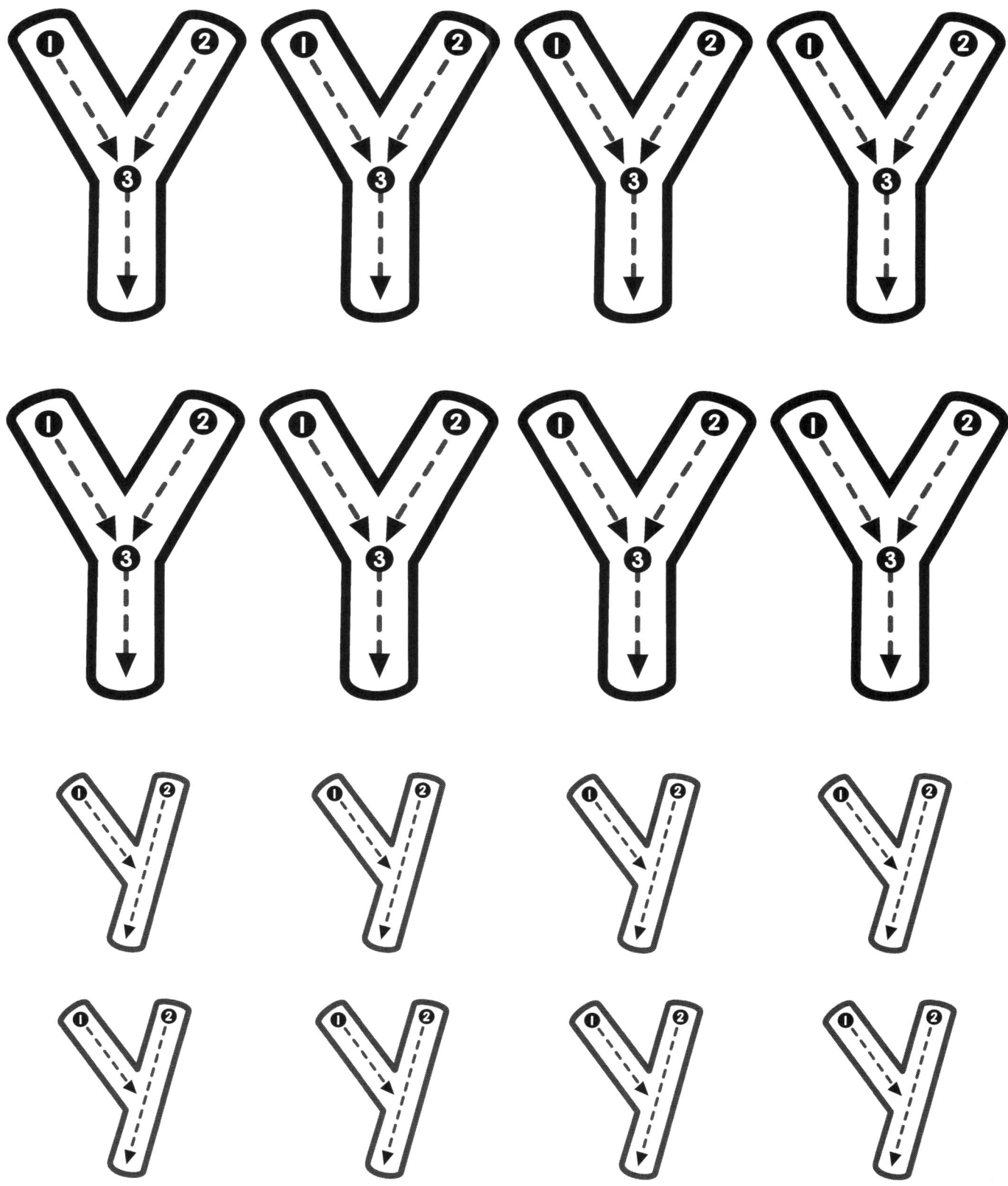

Yak

LETTER Z

Zebra

THE ALPHABET

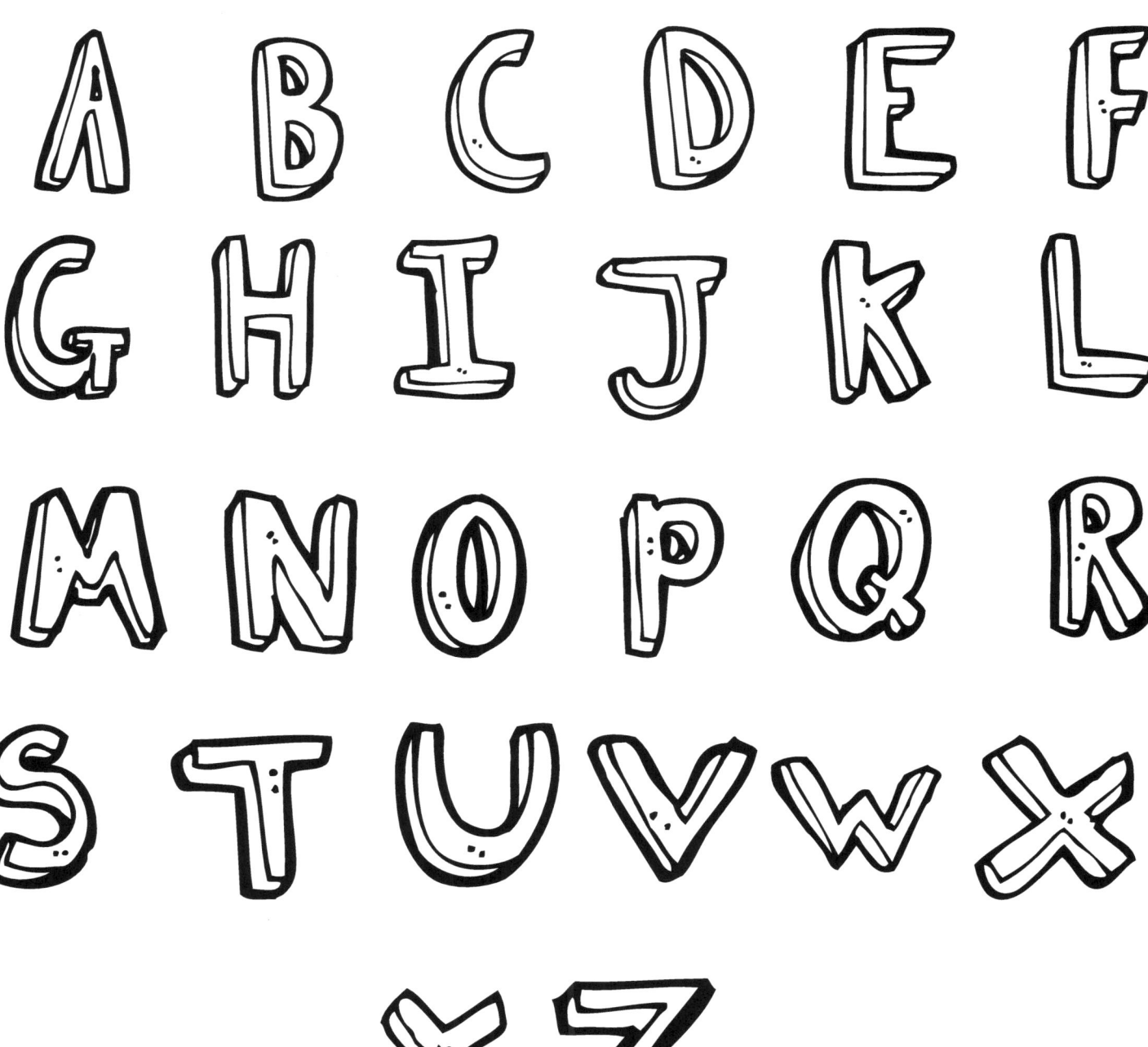

Made in the USA
Columbia, SC
02 May 2023

15961487R00059